THE STORY OF WOMAN

THE
MOUNTAIN

JUDE DOWNES

First published 2019

Text copyright © Jude Downes 2019
The moral right of the author has been asserted
Cover artwork by Geoffrey Downes

All rights reserved. No part of this publication may be reproduced, stored in a retrieval system, or transmitted in any form or by any means, electronic, mechanical, photocopying, recording or otherwise, without the prior written permission of the publisher and copyright holder.

A self published title designed and produced by Adala Publishing
www.adalapublishing.com.au

ISBN 978-0-6485272-3-7 (Print)
ISBN 978-0-6485272-4-4 (eBook)
ISBN 978-0-6485272-5-1 (PDF)

www.judedownes.com

Contents

Introduction	1
The Mountain	3
A New Trail	9
The Tribe of Woman	13
Signposts	17
Let Go	21
Remember the Dreams	25
Be in the Moment	29
Trust	33
A Sacred Detour	37
Find your Light	41
Courage	45
Enter the Womb of Creation	49
You are Never Alone	53

Choices	57
Opportunities	61
Ceremony	65
Wisdom	69
Take a Journey into the Unknown	71
Reach for the Stars	73
Crystal Guides	77
Honour your Journey	81
Sanctuary	85
It's All about Love	89
Keep Going	93
The Child Within	97
Twin Hearts	101
Birth	107
Worth	111
Laughter	115
Be a Leader	119
The Saboteur	123
Stay Focused on the Present	127
Matriarchal Support	133
The Pinnacle	137

Introduction

THE WORLD OF story opens our heart and soul to recognise the truth within. Story touches us with profound words. I am a 'Healer with Words', setting the scene for the story of Woman as she takes a journey up the metaphorical mountain, learning her lessons, facing challenges, accepting love. Words carry a vibration and when we work with storytelling, we trigger healing within us and mechanisms for guiding us on our journey.

When you journey along with Woman through each chapter, you journey with your soul, to access the aspect of the trail you most need to work with right now.

There are no spreads to guide a sequence. There is just one chapter at a time to work with, when you need to, in order to learn something about your journey.

This Story of Woman is a story of journeying, of healing, of trust and of new birth.

The purpose of everything I write is to create a new chapter in your life story or assist you in navigating your current chapter. I love the power of story to guide us on our way through life.

Work with *The Story of Woman – The Mountain* for self-exploration on your own journey. It is also a wonderful tool for healers to use in their healing practice with clients. Or perhaps work with it in your sacred circle group or as a meditation. There is a myriad of ways to work with these beautiful stories. Story touches your soul and can be a catalyst for change. The series of messages from the *Story of Woman* books can be a unique guide on your journey.

Come on a journey with me in Book One of the *Story of Woman* series.

Empowering Women to Empower Themselves.

With love

Jude

HOW TO WORK WITH THE STORYTELLER

The Mountain

WE ALL HAVE mountains to climb in life. We start at the bottom and weave our way around the mountain trail, learning, gathering wisdom, facing challenges, and creating a journey of understanding about who we are in life, and what we have to offer. Our personal mountains are part of a greater mountain range that others are also climbing at their own pace.

As you work with these stories, you will discover that a chapter may come to you over and over and so you look at what the story is expressing within your own life that perhaps requires some inner transformation or healing. Our stories are multi-layered and as such we will revisit these aspects of the journey from time to time.

When we complete a journey up one mountain, we have an opportunity to rest awhile before we begin the next journey. When you come to the final chapter, take the opportunity to look at the vista before you and see the victories you have achieved along the journey.

THE TRAIL

Our trail through life has many twists and turns. So often, we have no idea what is coming for us around the next curve in the trail. This is where we need to trust and know we can handle what comes for us in our own unique way.

The chapters in the *The Story of Woman* series are metaphors and symbols for the journey. As you go within to meditate or contemplate the journey ahead, you will understand how it applies to your own life.

THE MESSAGE

The message is a guide to help you understand your journey and offer wisdom from the Ancient Ones about your trail through life. It is a message to provide you with encouragement and empowering words to help you journey in the moment.

THE STORY

Storytelling has a way of touching something deep within us. Metaphoric storytelling helps us see an overview of life, often striking a chord offering special aha moments. Creating stories as metaphors is a magical way of engaging the reader in a journey they can recognise as their own. The healing power of these spiritual stories can be transformative. They tap into the heart and touch something profoundly deep within you, to heal a story or to acknowledge the power reflected in your own journey. These beautiful chapters in *The Story of Woman* ignite the imagination without getting into the rationalities of thought. Anything is possible in the imagination, but there is always a truth held within words that speak of the everyday journey in an extraordinary way.

I call it story-weaving as we are truly weaving our imaginative threads into tangible ways of navigating this journey through life. Each chapter in the *The Story of Woman* series weaves together her fears, doubts, love and joy as she journeys ever upward to stand at the top of her personal mountain, and to bear witness to the journey of those around her as she takes in the beautiful vista to which we all have access.

You are the protagonist in your own story. You come across antagonists in your life who help you grow through the challenges they present. Ultimately the key is to discover a beautiful and powerful resolution.

In each chapter in this bigger story, you *are* Woman, the protagonist. The antagonists are the challenges and the resolution is your understanding. Apply it as an overlay to your own everyday story and you will move forward in the direction you want to head.

PUTTING IT ALL TOGETHER

When you receive your *Story of Woman* book, hold it between your hands and then against your heart and claim this book as your own personal guide, or as a guide in your healing practice.

1. Read *The Story of Woman* from beginning to end and feel her journey. There will be chapters you resonate with right now.
2. Allow your intuition to choose the chapter you need to explore. Read through the Contents and see or feel which chapter and its message is the one you need to work with at this time.
3. You may choose to work with your pendulum or just be guided by your intuition. Perhaps open *The Story of Woman* randomly to see where you are guided at this moment.

4. You may wish to ask a question about your own life before choosing your chapter or perhaps just ask what you need to know right now.

This journey is one of trusting which chapter is the one for you. One chapter at a time is all you need to work with as they all contain powerful messages of transformation. Each chapter represents a part of the way up the trail of your personal mountain.

If you are working with *The Story of Woman* in your healing practice, allow your client to choose the chapter with which to work. It is a wonderful tool to either begin the healing journey, or finish the journey to tie up where you have been.

If you are working in a sacred circle, choose one chapter for the group either at the beginning of the circle or perhaps at the end to weave the threads of your journey together. Or you may like to encourage women to choose their own chapter so that each woman in the group is one part of the greater story of your circle.

However you choose to work with *The Story of Woman*, enjoy the journey.

CHAPTER 1

A New Trail

WOMAN IS READY to begin her walk up the mountain. However, she stands in stillness for a few moments at its base as she takes in the sheer magnitude of the journey ahead. Life has been nudging her to create change for some time and willingly, or perhaps in reality a little unwillingly, she now she finds herself standing at the base of this mountain looking upward.

She cannot see the peak of this mountain as it's hidden in the mist. She has no idea how far she needs to climb. She has no idea what is waiting for her along the trail, let alone what is at the top, but she does know that this new adventure is exciting and perhaps a little risky at times.

It is probably more than a little scary in places and yet her intuition is pushing her to take this next trail.

Woman looks down at the earth beneath her feet, aware that a narrow trail is ahead of her. Dense bush and trees partially cover this trail so that she can only see a little way ahead. Woman will need to rely on all of her senses if she is to take this journey. She certainly cannot see the top of the mountain, the ultimate destination.

This journey is going to take a lot of trust. She turns to look at the path from where she has just come. Woman realises that the path she has taken up until now has prepared the way for the trail ahead up the mountain. She glances left and then right and sees her guides, her guardians standing beside her ready to walk with her. They are ready to share her journey as she takes this next trail. Woman knows she will never be alone as together, they take the first steps forward upon this narrow trail, one step at a time. Excitement is building for the adventure ahead. There is no time like now to begin as the new moon is offering new light on a new trail.

MESSAGE

Never be afraid to begin a new journey. Regardless of your chronological age, you are never too young or too old to begin the next adventure. This life is a learning curve and the more we learn, the more exciting the trail becomes. This is a time of looking at the opportunities to move on to a new trail that is presenting itself to you.

CHAPTER 2

The Tribe of Woman

WOMAN DONS HER backpack of what she perceives are necessary things she needs for the journey and walks forward. The trail is already narrow and the undergrowth is so thick in parts that Woman needs to climb over it or push it back in order to journey forward. Her guides explain to her that this is *her* journey and they are with her for support, to offer wisdom when needed or to guide her in the direction she needs to go. However, they will not interfere with the journey. In the beginning Woman thought the only way forward was straight up. However, she has since discovered that her trail weaves around the mountain making the journey a little easier going than she first envisaged. First lesson of this new journey is that the trails of life are not necessarily as fearsome as they might appear to be in her mind.

Woman's trail seems to be coming to a clearing and her guidance offers her the opportunity to rest for a time. There is a fireplace in the centre of this clearing and it looks like it has been built recently in readiness for her arrival. Is it even possible that someone would know that she would be here and ready for a rest? Yes, say her guides. This is your trail through life and there are many who are in tune with you. Many who desire to help you along the way.

Woman picks up the matches alongside the fire and soon there is a blazing warm fire for her to sit beside. She is lulled into the quiet and stillness of this place, this clearing. All she can hear is the crackle of the fire and feel its nourishing warmth on her skin.

She muses to herself that her second lesson is to trust that there are those who want to help her on her journey in life. She needs to observe and accept help when needed. She doesn't have to journey on her own anymore. Woman gazes into the fire and sees her tribe dancing together in the flames. She smiles to herself, she is not alone, Woman is loved and supported.

MESSAGE

You are never alone in life. It may appear that way at times. However, you are always surrounded by your team in spirit. You are well supported on your journey. Talk with your inner guidance often and trust your inner wise messages. They are fuelled with love for the journey. This is a time to seek out your soul tribe. They are closer than you think.

CHAPTER 3

Signposts

WOMAN HAS RECOGNISED her second lesson and the trail is opening up now to be wider and kinder to her journey. The undergrowth has receded somewhat. It is time to relieve herself of the backpack she has carried with her on this journey. There are many things Woman thinks she needs to carry with her. Things she is sure she cannot do without: feelings, thoughts, old hurts, life conditioning. She has packed them up into a neat backpack to take with her on her new trail.

The trail winds around the mountain but it is still uphill and even though the trail has widened somewhat and is not nearly as harsh, the backpack is getting heavy. With each step, her guidance is asking her to relieve herself of her burdens, to leave them behind. Woman has fought hard to hold on to these life experiences, these old stories. To let them go is a scary thing. In her peripheral vision, Woman can see that there are signposts dotted along the edges of the trail. She would like to stop and see what they are about, but her heavy backpack means that to stop on this uphill journey would break her momentum and it would be difficult to get going again.

Her guidance offers advice once more. Drop the backpack or miss the signposts that offer wisdom for the journey. Woman realises now that the signposts are meant for her, placed there deliberately to show her the way along the trail. If only she will slow the journey long enough to read them, to work on the clues left for her by her higher guides to encourage the way forward. What has she been missing along the way she wonders? Does she need to go back and begin the journey again? Woman asks herself if she can truly let go of the backpack and is she really ready to step forward into the unknown without it? Is she strong enough to make the journey without it?

MESSAGE

As you follow the signposts that life offers you, you will see a clear trail ahead. Often it is the repetition of signs of which we take the most notice. What signposts are coming into your awareness now? Create your own story around what you see. These signposts are symbols and as such, are the language of your soul. Interpretation of the signposts will come from trust as you weave the story of their meaning into your everyday life.

CHAPTER 4

Let Go

FINALLY LAYING HER backpack down on the ground, Woman steps to the side of her trail to the signpost that is standing so straight and tall. It almost seems to be glowing. How did she not notice these signposts before? Even before she has finished voicing her question, she is aware of the answer. She has been so busy lugging the old stories with her in her neat little backpack and feeling the pain of their weight upon her back and shoulders, that she wasn't truly aware of anything else around her.

Her guidance stands quietly by, proud of her for stopping and laying down her burden. Proud of her for taking a step towards wisdom, towards spiritual enlightenment, that will help on her everyday journey.

Woman looks over and around the signpost, and at first, it just appears to be the usual signpost, offering limited information about heading the right way. Disappointed, she steps back a little to gain a better perspective on what her guides have indicated is important to her journey.

As Woman retreats just a little to see the overall picture in front of her, the signpost glows a little brighter and in her heart and her soul she knows, without a doubt, the next step on her journey. Woman acknowledges the signpost that is hers alone and smiles at the simplicity of the message received and integrated into her heart space. There is no need for words or actions. It is as simple as opening her heart to the possibilities offered to her by stopping her journey awhile, laying down her burden and being willing to explore the signposts along her trail.

She turns to pick up her backpack. It is still lying where she left it. Her guidance is standing beside it and asks, 'do you really want to carry this backpack any further along this new trail?' Woman shakes her head. She has something new and exciting happening in her life and she has no time to carry the wounds of the stories long past. Her guidance nods imperceptibly and her backpack fades from view. Her guidance tells her that should she wish to pick it up again anywhere along the trail, she is certainly welcome to. The choice is hers to make. However, it truly is no longer necessary to haul it along on the journey ahead.

Lesson number three has just been shown to her. In order to see the signposts along the trails of life one must lay down the backpack filled with old stories that are no longer relevant to the journey, or take a chance and carry it and miss out on the fabulous signposts that guide the way. She will always have a choice.

MESSAGE

Lay down your backpack of troubles for a little while and test how it feels not to carry them around with you all of the time. What do you notice that is different in your life? What do you see that you couldn't while carrying that backpack around? Now that you are focusing on you in this moment, what is changing? You do not have to take *everything* forward with you on your journey.

CHAPTER 5

Remember the Dreams

WOMAN IS LIGHTER without her backpack of old stories, her step is surer. The trail is winding its way around the mountain and she can only see as far as the next curve. The surface of the trail keeps changing. Sometimes smooth, sometimes a little rough, but all in all, the trail seems relatively easy going now and she is feeling confident as her stride lengthens to match her mood. Woman rounds the next curve and sees there are large rocks strewn across the trail as though a rockfall has placed them there. Actually, Woman thinks, they are more like huge boulders. How will I get through them?

Woman ponders her predicament. She thought that after the narrow path and dense bush at the beginning of the trail, the lessons learned along the way, the letting go of her backpack of old stories and welcoming a signpost to point her in the right direction, that the trail would become much easier. Why then is the trail covered in rocks too big to move?

Her guidance stands beside her, quietly waiting for her to find the answer within. Woman finally realises she needs to ask a question first. Why did the rocks fall across her trail? They don't look like they have been there long as the dust is still settling. The answer doesn't lie in the 'how' of moving the rocks or navigating her way around or over them, it really is a question of why are they there in the first place.

Woman steps away from the trail to observe the rocks, to feel their energy. This block in the trail of life has derailed her forward momentum. The question eludes her for a moment or two.

Woman's guidance offers a hint. What are your dreams? Woman wonders what her dreams have to do with this block on the trail and then, understanding comes. Her dreams are about what she wants and needs to create in her life for fulfilment, for joy and happiness, for purpose. Before she undertook this new journey, she was thinking about what she wanted to create in her life. When she began her journey along this mountain trail she cast aside her dream, thinking herself not worthy of attaining it, thinking dreams belonged in the world of others, thus creating a block, *this* block, in the trail.

Woman thought this trail would offer a smooth new journey to somewhere, anywhere and she would give up her dream forever.

Woman's understanding of this fourth lesson is that all who seek their trail are worthy of living their dreams, and understanding that will offer a solution to move through the block in the trail. Woman knows now that she must never give up her dream.

Now she has an understanding, the solution appears in front of her. Woman notices a tiny path just before the rocks, a detour that will likely take her around the fallen rocks, the block. It is a side adventure she is ready to take. Her guidance is satisfied Woman has learned the lesson of worthiness well. Together, they walk off the main trail and into the next adventure.

MESSAGE

Never give up on your dreams. Over time they may change direction. They may look a little different to your first image of them, but the dream is always valid. Dreams are the realm of the imagination and can be as grand as you make them. Now is the time to set some achievable goals so that you can take the next step towards achieving your dream. Each goal achieved not only brings your dream a little closer, it also alters the form of your dream. This is personal growth at its best!

CHAPTER 6

Be in the Moment

THE TRACK LEADS down into a deep gully, a sacred place that links the many mountains around her. Woman's soft footfalls muffle her journey. Large ferns and tall trees create a dark mysterious canopy. Birds high in the treetops are the only sounds Woman can hear. She walks mindfully down this narrow track.

Woman begins to hear rustling in the ferns beside her bringing more than a little fear to this adventure. The unknown has always been a little bit of a scary place to live for Woman.

She thinks back to the rocks blocking her trail and knows that the only way to navigate her way around them is to take this tiny side track deep into the gully, away from the main trail and into the unknown. Her heart is pounding. She is not sure whether it's just fear, or if excitement is also part of this journey.

The deeper she journeys, the quieter within she becomes. She is not aware of anything much except her own beating heart. No thoughts are invading her mind. As she places one foot in front of the other, any residual fears are replaced by this quiet. Trust in her journey is intuitive. Her guides are ever present and also quiet.

A new sound comes to her. Water running over rocks. The further she journeys, the more she not only hears the water but also feels its powerful energy pulling her toward its source.

The track Woman is detouring along flattens out as she reaches the bottom of the gully. Woman discovers she is standing at the edge of a stream, a crystal-clear stream. The sound of water running over rocks is actually a narrow high waterfall. The spray is creating a beautiful rainbow arc as it falls onto the rocks below before entering the stream to flow wherever it allows itself to flow.

Woman sits beside the stream, dipping her feet into the water, watching colourful fish swimming around. She listens to the sounds of the water, feeling the soft earth beneath her.

She doesn't know what the next step might be right now and that is perfectly okay. Woman knows this lesson is one of merely being in the beauty of this moment. Nothing more, nothing less, nothing to fear. Simply being in the moment and noticing everything around her, Woman fought her natural instinct to fear this side track, but she knew the way to move forward on her trail was to take it or turn back. Taking a chance on it has brought her to a beautiful place. She can't even think about what might come next.

MESSAGE

When you live in the moment, you see what is around you. The beauty of life that exists both within and without is identifiable because you are not visiting some future place or diving into past journeys. You do not always need to know the next step before you take it. Sometimes the unknown will bring the greatest beauty.

CHAPTER 7

Trust

TIME PASSES IN the beauty and quiet of this sacred place. Woman has learned so much on this journey already. There is still so far to go but she feels ready to return to the main trail.

Her guides begin to speak. 'You cannot return the way you came as the rocks still block the trail, therefore, the only way forward is via this detour and into the waterfall, or give up and turn back on the trail altogether.' Woman looks at her guides and can see they are serious. It seems she is to take another journey into the unknown. Woman had thought that she would sit in her stillness awhile and the rocks on her main trail would magically disappear, and she would continue her journey. It seems that is not the case. But into the waterfall? What is coming now?

'A test,' they say. Oh no, thinks Woman. Will I pass it? 'If you want to, you will,' they reply.

Woman looks towards the waterfall, however, she cannot see anything. 'Open your vision,' her guides instruct. 'Look deeper, further.' Woman does as she is asked and eventually sees a cave beyond the falling water. So, she ponders, she is to enter a frightening cave of unknown content. It is also high up. How is she to reach it she wonders? 'Why you climb of course,' they reply.

Woman stands on the edge of the stream looking at the waterfall. She observes the best way to climb. It appears slippery with water spilling all over the rocks at the entrance of the cave.

'Look again,' her guides offer. Opening her sight beyond the ordinary, Woman sees a series of hand and footholds that are well worn, as though many have made this journey before her. Trust, Woman thinks to herself. Trust. I've got this. Woman begins to climb until she stands behind the waterfall at the entrance to a very dark cave.

Woman notes that some of the big lessons here involve trust and careful observation beyond the ordinary. However, is she willing to step into the darkness of what lays ahead of her? The choice is hers to make. Return to the main trail and turn back, or conquer her fear of the unknown and journey forward on this detour to the other side of the rockfall, the block in the trail and continue her journey.

MESSAGE

You can want and dream and scheme all you like, however, until you learn the lesson of trust in the journey, it will remain a dream. Have you ever felt that nudge within that is attempting to move you forward, but you resist because you feel you don't have all the pieces, all the knowledge yet? This is a time to look at what that nudge is trying to show you and ask, 'Okay, what do you want me to do?' Trust is key to unlocking doors of opportunity and growth.

CHAPTER 8

A Sacred Detour

WOMAN KNOWS THAT this cave, situated deep down in a sacred gully, along a narrow track will ultimately lead her back to her main trail once more as she navigates her way around the block, which was the reason she needed to take this detour.

She turns and faces the entrance to the cave and peers into the inky darkness. Her heart is pounding loudly in her ears. Woman wonders what challenges lie ahead in the darkness.

She calls to her guides as she wonders if there's something they need to tell her, to share with her about this cave? 'No,' they say. 'This is your journey, and we are by your side. All we can tell you right now is that this is the journey of the Goddess within.'

Taking a deep breath, Woman takes her first step across the threshold of the cave, and then another step, and then another and another. She stops and lets her eyes adjust to the darkness, however, she can still only see around her immediate vicinity. She turns a little to look back at the entrance to the cave. There is light shining from beyond the waterfall. Turning forward again, she peers into the darkness. What has she undertaken? She is not a quitter, but this almost seems beyond her as her fear of the unknown wells up from deep within and threatens to overflow and disempower her, sending her racing back to the light at the entrance.

Woman stands almost rooted to the spot. What should she do now she questions? 'Find your light,' she hears in her mind and heart. 'When you are standing in the darkness, find your light and you will see.'

Where did that come from, she wonders?

Woman stands for a few moments and decides that to 'find her light' is easier said than done. This new trail is challenging her more than she thought it would. Woman expected that by walking a new trail she could leave behind the old fears, doubts and challenges and start afresh. It seems that the lesson is not to expect anything. The lesson is to walk the trails of life and see what comes in the moment. It's so often the unexpected that arrives. Now, where is the light switch?

MESSAGE

There are times in life when you are shown a detour. Sometimes the detour is right for you and will assist you on your trails through life, and other times it is there as a distraction. This is a time to be discerning about the detour and weigh up whether you have created a distraction on your trail or whether this detour is worthy of your attention. Sit in the quiet of your heart space and take a journey into the beginnings of the detour and get a feel for it. This detour may offer you the tools needed to move through creative blocks in any area of your life. You will know if it is right for you at this time.

CHAPTER 9

Find your Light

WOMAN STANDS IN the stillness of the inner darkness and revisits the words she felt within more than heard. 'Find your light. When you are standing in the darkness, find your light and you will see.'

What does that mean, she wonders? Woman's intuition tells her to find the cave walls, but her fear of the unknown sees her shrink from reaching out to something she cannot see with her eyes. There could be anything horrible lying in wait for her. 'Look with your inner sight,' she hears. 'Look deeper, further. Remember that the way to truly see is to look beyond the obvious.'

Woman takes her focus inward and imagines what the cave walls might look like. She is surprised that she can easily see where the focus in her mind is aimed. There is nothing sinister waiting for her on those walls. However, there is a torch sitting in a sconce right beside her. All she needs to do is reach out, touch it and it will flame in her hands, lighting the world around her.

Woman hears a giggle, a woman's giggle. And then, 'Now you're getting the idea.'

Who *is* that? She asks in her mind. Woman looks to her guides but they just smile and shake their heads. Time will reveal all apparently. 'Look for the lesson,' is all they reply.

Woman stands in the stillness, and now the light she holds in her hand is bouncing shadows along the walls of the cave offering her light and shadow for the journey ahead. She still cannot see into the depths of the cave as the depths are, as yet, hidden from both her inner and outer view. Woman has learned to focus her intent, to trust what she sees with her inner vision, and that all she needs for the journey will be shown to her, in the right time, if she asks.

Even in the darkest of places she has found how to find the light by simply focusing and reaching out, and from that she has learned that she has all the tools needed to keep going. One final lesson here is that she doesn't need to know the whole trail in order to move into the deep recesses of life's journey. It's called trust.

Onward now and Woman begins to walk with confidence to the next part of her journey.

MESSAGE

In the dark recesses of life, you can always ignite your inner light. Fear cannot live where there is light. The key is to know your soul flame is still there inside you. This time is one of helping others to ignite their own inner flame so that together, you create more light in the world, your world. There may be a part of your life that has existed in the darkness for too long. When you shine your powerful and loving light on it, it can no longer hold the demons you thought were there. This is a healing journey.

CHAPTER 10

Courage

WOMAN WALKS DEEPER into the cave. The further she walks, the more confident she becomes. She can no longer see the entrance. Her torch is lighting enough of the world around her that she feels comfortable within herself. She is embraced in her own world, and it is as though nothing else exists beyond where her light shines. In reality, it does not exist. The outer world is only a memory, a thought.

Woman's heartbeat helps her keep a steady pace. Her fear of the unknown has been replaced with comfort. She knows only of what is immediately surrounding her. Even the shadows dancing on the walls hold no threat to her immediate existence.

She stops, as the energy in the cave is shifting. The dynamics of what she has become used to, seeing only what is around her, feeling only the quiet and closed nature of the cave, hearing only her own heartbeat, is changing.

Woman looks around her small lighted space. Everything looks pretty much the same and yet, there is something noticeably different. She trusts her intuition enough now to check in with herself to see if it is safe to journey on. There are no visible cues, therefore, the only way to know if the way forward is safe is to trust herself. Her guides are still with her, but they are silent, allowing her to take charge, to make her choices from a place of trust and inner knowing.

Woman feels the pull of an energy, that until now she has not been aware of. She hears the disembodied voice again, the one who had previously asked her to switch on her light, calling her closer, deeper into the cave.

Woman hears in her heart and soul, rather than in her mind, 'I am the Goddess and you are entering the womb of the Mother. Welcome.'

She catches her breath, feeling the warmth of the love from the Goddess deep within her. There is nothing to fear, there is only the joy of the sacred meeting to come.

MESSAGE

It takes courage and a lion-hearted spirit to release the fear of the unknown. This is a time to be in tune with your intuition so that you are courageous enough to continue the journey begun so long ago. Confidence is born of courage and you will discover more courage than you thought possible at the beginning of any new journey. Being courageous means that you can still feel the pangs of fear and go forward anyway. Love will offer courage for your journey.

CHAPTER 11

Enter the Womb of Creation

WHILE WOMAN WAS walking deep into the cave, her thoughts had become so quiet that she had no idea where she was going or what might be waiting for her ahead and it no longer mattered. Woman felt safe in her small lit space as she walked deep into the unknown. She thinks it is a comfortable place to be. What began in fear, became inner peace and acceptance. Woman understands now that all she needs to do is keep walking, be aware of her immediate world and she will open herself, her heart and mind to the magic that exists within her.

The pull of the Mother to enter the womb now runs deep. The energy is getting stronger and all of Woman's senses are on high alert. Something powerful is pulling her into a new world, a new way of being. Woman is aware that she is entering a different space within the narrow cave she has been walking.

Her light expands to take in a much larger space. She enters a vast cavern. This inner cavern is shaped like a womb with smooth sides dotted with all sorts of crystals and lit torches all around the walls. A smooth stone floor is carved with ancient symbols. Her soul recognises them as the symbols of the Ancient Ones, the Ones who walked this trail long ago. There is a remembering now that her trail in life is one walked by many before her.

Woman sighs as she knows this is a well-worn and now familiar trail. Her intuition followed the voice that spoke to her heart. She trusted the journey and overcame her fear of the unknown.

As she gazes around her, Woman looks to the centre of this womb-shaped space and fire is central in the space. Woman walks towards the fire and observes that laid out around it are sacred tools. There is a bowl of water, a feather, an unusual deck of cards with different symbols drawn on them, an obsidian crystal, a drum, and a wand.

In her heart and mind she hears, 'Sit beside the fire.' It is the same woman's voice who has instructed her on this inner cave journey. Curious and honouring the feeling deep within her that says trust, Woman sits beside the fire on a beautiful violet-coloured velvet cushion in a space that appears to have been waiting for her arrival. There is one other space opposite her. Woman waits in the quiet and eventually begins to look deeper, further, with her vision seeing beyond ordinary viewing.

Woman gasps at what she is seeing. It is not what she expected. But then, she thinks, nothing about her journey is ever what she expects. Her lesson, in this moment, is to be in the silence, and open her inner vision to what is possible, rather than just what appears on the surface.

MESSAGE

This is a time of rebirth; a time to enter the Cave of the Goddess, the metaphorical womb of the mother. You enter the womb to nourish yourself before you take another step on the trails of life. Your sacred inner fire is burning brightly, shining its light on the beauty of your life, as you wait for the right time to re-enter the world of the everyday. This is the time for gently nurturing yourself as you wait on the wise guidance of the Goddess within. Life is not always what it appears on the surface. When you open your inner vision to what is possible, you begin to witness the extraordinary overlaying the perceived ordinary.

CHAPTER 12

You are Never Alone

WOMAN OPENED HER everyday vision into something beyond the ordinary realm of existence, and what she can see is a world within a world. The Goddess is sitting opposite her, a beautiful, elegant woman of indeterminate age. There are animals, Elders, Angels and many things that she cannot begin to describe because, in her everyday world, they don't exist. The light is golden, showering everything with its shimmering glow. There are more crystals than she remembers upon entering the womb-like cavern, more symbols on the floor. There are cabinets with crystals and sacred tools. A pot of something pungent, but not unpleasant, is bubbling away in the shadows.

'I am the Goddess,' she hears in her heart. 'You are here because you accepted the challenge to move into the unknown, even when your heart knew fear.'

Woman gazes around and wonders at the beauty surrounding her in this inner world. The Goddess smiles at Woman. 'This, dear Woman is a time to be reborn and take up your tools for the journey ahead. You are to journey out of the cave and back onto your trail. You trusted your own journey and arrived here to be immersed in love and empowerment, and to remember the journey ahead.'

'This inner realm is as much a part of your everyday life as that which is mundane. The time of remembering who you are as Woman, as a Wise Warrior Woman is now.'

'You have more guidance than you know, including the Ancient Ones, your ancestors, who walked this trail long ago. The tools you see around this fire are sacred to you. Tools you have worked with in many lifetimes. They are returned to you now to assist you on the journey ahead.'

Woman is silent, remembering now the ancient trails. Her heart fills with joy, love, and hope. This trail is about to take a new turn; one she did not expect and she couldn't be happier.

Closing her eyes for a moment, Woman tries to commit everything she has seen to memory. She hears the voice of the Goddess once more. 'The memory of this time and place lives in your heart. That is all you need.' Woman opens her eyes and the scene in front of her has returned to the fire and her sacred tools. She is alone.

Woman hears. 'You are never alone on the journey of life. Now that you are remembering who you are, you will feel the presence of your guides when you are in touch with the alternate nature and duality of life's journey.'

Woman gathers her sacred tools and prepares to return to her trail as she thinks about her lesson here. The heart always remembers the journey even when the mind forgets. Something to contemplate on the journey now.

MESSAGE

When the trail appears tough, your inner guidance will show you the way if you trust and call upon it to assist you. Some will hear their guidance with their inner hearing. Some will just know without knowing how they know. Others will hear through their heart and the feelings evoked. Some will follow the signposts placed along their path and *all* ways are right for that person. This is a time to listen to your inner wise guides. They offer valuable guidance about the next steps to take on your journey.

CHAPTER 13

Choices

WOMAN'S BACKPACK APPEARS again, but now it is empty and ready to be filled with her sacred tools. Filling it, Woman notices there is room for plenty more to be added along the journey of her life.

Woman gazes around the womb-like cavern once more, feeling safe and loved and knowing she is on the right trail for her. As Woman looks around her, she wonders if she is supposed to return the way she came or if there's another opening for her to follow.

Her guides appear by her side and tell her that she cannot return to her trail through the same way. They indicate that there are several openings off this cavern that she hadn't noticed before. She is to choose one. Woman sighs and wonders out loud why they can't just point her to the right one.

Her guides smile and say, 'All of the entrances will lead you back onto your trail. Each is a tunnel likened to a birth canal. Your intuition will lead you to the one that is right for you, right now.'

Woman stands and wonders why it just can't be easy and why can't they just tell her the way. They chuckle and tell her, 'We are your guides who agreed to assist you on your journey in this lifetime. We are here to encourage you to make your own intuitive choices, and this is one of them.'

'Once again, look deeper and further than your ordinary vision to know which choice is the right one for you. We offer guidance on how to find the way rather than tell you the way.'

This makes perfect sense to Woman, knowing that they are teaching her self-reliance and trust while offering spiritual guidance on how to find her way on this trail in life.

Opening up her spiritual vision, Woman looks at the different openings around her. All feel right, and for a moment she panics. She has a need to make the right choice as old thoughts and feelings say she doesn't want to make a mistake. 'You cannot make a mistake,' her guides tell her. 'It is about choice and trust. The way that is right for you, right now, will be shown to you.'

Woman takes a deep breath and one opening in particular, is shining a little brighter than the others. She strides quickly forward, shoulders back, without allowing any challenging thoughts to enter her mind. Woman shrugs her backpack filled with her sacred tools onto her shoulders and walks into the opening, down a narrow tunnel, a kind of birth canal, and back out onto her trail and the openness of the world around her. Looking to her right, she notes the boulders, the blocks, have gone. Her trail is clear in both directions. Turning left towards the upward trail, Woman sets off on the next part of her journey. It is almost the full moon, and she wonders what life has in store for her.

MESSAGE

There are many trails to choose from and each road offered will guide you to where you need to be. Each trail will offer a unique lesson on your journey. The key is to trust the right trail for you. This may not always be the easiest trail to follow, but it will be the wisest choice because you chose it from a place of trust in your guides, in conjunction with the wise inner self. We make choices in life all the time, but so often we do not trust the bigger choices. There is just choice and relying on self to make the right one will feel like you are entering the birth canal and re-entering the world, your world, with renewed vigour and love for the journey.

CHAPTER 14

Opportunities

WOMAN SETS OUT on her trail, her backpack of sacred tools light on her back. The sun is setting, and the moon is on the rise. It is a night of the full moon Woman realises, but she is not yet ready to stop. Woman feels the pull of the earth beneath her and the pull of the rising moon.

Woman's guides ask her to stop to rest but Woman insists she should keep going. Her guides tell her that she can certainly make that choice, if that is what she intuitively feels, however, it would perhaps be wise to sit a while, open her backpack and retrieve one of her sacred tools.

Woman is concerned she is about to miss an opportunity for something special if she does not continue to follow the energy beneath her feet and the rising moon. Her guides tell her that she cannot miss out on what is her opportunity to take. Taking some time to stop and look into something can only enhance her journey.

Woman concedes this is likely the truth so she sits, takes off her backpack and reaches her hand inside. It is the deck of cards with ancient symbols on them that she draws out of her pack.

She sits quietly for a few moments, asking what she needs to become aware of right now. Carefully shuffling the deck, one card flies out and lands face up on the earth in front of her. There is no book for an explanation, however, she knows it. Her heart remembers the symbol from long ago when she walked the earth as one of the Ancients. It is the symbol of ceremony. Woman looks to her guides and acknowledges their help. She is aware that if she had not stopped as suggested, she would not have known about the need for ceremony on this full moon. She would likely have missed this opportunity, searching instead for something she had no idea about. Her ego was getting in the way of the journey, looking for other ways of receiving the information needed, Woman's guides are teaching her to become aware of the many ways wisdom and knowledge can be experienced.

Holding the card with its symbol against her heart, she hears drumming and chanting. Woman knows exactly where she needs to be. She packs the card away and places the deck into her backpack before shouldering the pack once more. Ceremony is calling her. The moon is yet to reach its zenith. Her lesson is one of not being so dogged about completing her journey that she fails to take time to sit and just be in the moment.

MESSAGE

Sometimes you need to stop in your tracks and listen to your heart. If you push through and keep going when your heart says stop and listen for a moment, you might miss an opportunity that will take you on another fabulous journey. Take a breather now and then, and trust that stopping is often the key to moving forward. This is a time to recalibrate your energies and once again, trust what your heart is trying to tell you. The right opportunity will never pass you by if you are prepared to stop and listen awhile. You are more likely to miss it if you keep pushing on. An opportunity to grow something is coming to you now.

CHAPTER 15

Ceremony

WOMAN WALKS TOWARDS the sounds of the drums and chanting, each footstep bringing her closer, her heart beating strongly in time with the drumming. Will they allow her to join in their ceremony, whoever *they* are, she wonders?

The sounds are close now. The moon is almost at its highest point. There is a narrow gap in the rocks just to the side of the trail. Another detour she thinks, but when she steps through the rocks, a large open space is filled with women of many different nationalities all standing in a circle. They turn collectively, still drumming and chanting and beckon her to join them.

There is one space in the circle of women directly in front of her. Woman realises that this space is just for her and the women have been expecting her arrival. They are all ages, from Ancient Ones to younger women. Woman does not question how these beautiful women knew of her impending arrival. This is the magic of working with spirit.

Ceremony has just begun, and she senses that her presence now completes the circle of women. The drumming increases; the chanting is louder now. Woman takes her drum from her backpack and begins to beat in time with the other women. She intuitively knows the chant and adds her voice to the many. The vibration of this sacred time and place is palpable, vibrant, alive. A fire crackles and roars in the centre of the circle and in her heart and mind she understands that fire is central to everything. It is the soul fire of creation. The full moon is now directly overhead. The women begin to move slowly around the circle, dancing rhythmically. Drumming, chanting, thinking clear pure thoughts of creative intention, ever grateful for the journey of sisters. Woman is grateful for the knowledge that her dreaming story, since she began the journey on the new moon, has the light of the full moon shining upon it, with love. Ceremony is always the beginning of a new journey of awareness. There is no time but right now. Woman is learning just how precious and good life can be. Woman is content.

MESSAGE

Creating a sacred ceremony allows for new intentions to be set. Keep your focus strong. This is a time to be with your sisterhood of friends and family. Add your sacred voice to the voices of women rising up all over the world as they embrace the Divine Feminine Spirit. Chant, sing, dance, write and speak prayers of intent or whatever raises your vibration to enter into ceremony. You are loved and welcomed by the Ancient Ones as they encourage you to take your place with others seeking the way forward.

CHAPTER 16

Wisdom

CEREMONY IS COMPLETE and the circle is closed. Woman can see one of the Ancient Ones approaching her. Woman waits and feels that she is about to take another fork in the road. So much is happening for her on this journey of life. So many lessons. So many twists and turns and detours. She wonders how she can keep up with the energies offered to her. Woman can only trust the journey.

The Ancient One stands in front of her, resplendent in robes of gold, silver, and violet. Her silver hair reaches down her back; a small crystal crown is her only adornment. Her eyes are the same violet as her robe. Her generous smile encouraging.

'Come,' she invites, 'the others are waiting.' Woman thinks she must be mistaking her for someone else as her manner implies familiarity. Woman is sure they have not previously met. The smile widens, and the Ancient One reaches out her hand to take Woman's in hers. 'Come,' she repeats.

Woman has just been in sacred ceremony with all of the women here so, in trust, she feels she must go with her. However, not without a little trepidation. Opening her heart and mind a little, Woman peers into the depths of the eyes of the Ancient One and what she sees is the wisdom of the cosmos deep within them. Woman takes a sharp intake of breath because that brief glimpse is already opening up her imagination, with the ability to see beyond her ordinary world.

MESSAGE

There is a difference between following someone or something just because it seems like a good idea and *really* knowing the wisdom of what you are doing, truly is right for you, right now. Do what you know is right for you, rather than letting someone talk you into doing something that isn't quite the right fit for you. There is something sacred waiting for you when you look deeply into what is presenting itself and discover that it sets your heart fluttering with joy.

CHAPTER 17

Take a Journey into the Unknown

'WHAT IF I told you,' the Ancient One begins, 'that you can reach for the stars and touch them with your heart and mind.' Woman considers the question carefully, wanting to answer correctly. It seems the Ancient One is reading her mind. 'There is no wrong answer, just believe in what is possible.'

Woman replies that she has only thought about her journey in earthly terms and even though this journey is a spiritual one, she cannot comprehend that she can also journey to the stars.

'We, the Ancient Ones, honour you and your journey. You once walked this earth and the stars as one of us.'

Woman and the Ancient One had been walking and talking for some time and Woman did not realise they had stopped walking until the Ancient One at her side said, 'Look around you.'

They had walked to a place of standing stones. Within the circle of stones stood other Ancient Ones, each one taking up a position in front of a stone. There are two places left. Her ancient guide indicates one of the stones is for her to stand and she will take up the final position. Woman wonders where she is to journey now. She closes her eyes, not sure she is ready for another mysterious magical tour, so she leans against her stone for support as the ground beneath her feet appears to give way. Her final thought as she heads on this next adventure is that she will never come to the end of her life and die wondering what adventure might feel like.

MESSAGE

You are supported on your journey into the unknown. When you are ready to take a leap of faith, the unknown will become known. The ground beneath you may give way just before you head off on another adventure, but it is time to trust you have all the guidance you need to help you through the shifting sands of life.

CHAPTER 18

Reach for the Stars

WOMAN LEANS INTO her stone in the circle of the Ancient Ones as the earth beneath her feet no longer feels like solid ground. In her mind and her heart, she hears, 'We are of the stars and the old ways.' The Ancient Ones say, 'We are one of the many old ones who walked the earth eons ago. We are the ones who oversee the seeding of light within those who agreed, so long ago, to awaken at this time.'

Woman takes a deep breath and dares to open her eyes. She gasps as she sees whirling energy in front of her, all around her. This whirling energy is light, and she watches the energy build. The Ancient Ones and the stones begin to disappear, appearing to become one with the light. Woman hears a chuckle. 'We are all indeed light,' she hears. 'When consciousness vibrates high enough, the body appears to drop away, and we become pure light, melding with the One, the source of the light.'

Woman feels quiet within. There is nothing but peace that exists in this light-filled vortex. 'You are the earth. You are the stars. You are the light.' This is the message of the Ancient Ones. As the light whirls faster, it feels like Woman is standing still. She closes her eyes again to feel the presence of the oneness and peace rolls over her and through her once more.

'You can tap into the wisdom of the light, to take others on a journey to places that are, as yet, unknown to them. Open your eyes,' Woman is instructed, 'and see.'

Woman opens her eyes, and the whirling vortex of light is now filled with galaxies held in the beauty of the light. New stars are being born. Suns, moons, and planets rotate within the vortex. Woman is in awe of this scene but silently wonders why she is witnessing this beautiful spectacle. The Ancient Ones explain. 'All of humanity has a sacred gift to share with others. This is the order of things. Now is the time for each person to remember their gift, to awaken the sleeping gift within. It is time to share that gift with others so that transformational magic, in the form of sacred gifts, can change the status quo in the outer world.'

Awareness is coming into the consciousness of Woman. Her gift is to encourage others to reach for the stars and to believe in the magic of the inner world, to create change from within, to assist a crumbling external world.

She has entered into the cave and accepted her sacred tools for the journey. She has moved creative blocks. She has been part of a sacred ceremony and journeyed to the stars with the Ancient Ones. Her rich inner world will reflect into her outer world in ways she cannot possibly yet know. All Woman knows, is that trust is a big part of her journey.

MESSAGE

When you are ready to reach for the proverbial stars, you will fly higher in your sacred journeying than ever before. Your gift in this lifetime will be remembered. This is a time of remembering why you came here at this time and your purpose of the now. Remembering that you are one with everything will open doors of opportunity and connections beyond what you thought possible. This is your time of remembering the beauty of self and how that beauty will weave its magic in life.

CHAPTER 19

Crystal Guides

WOMAN IS ONCE more on her trail on the sacred mountain. She reflects on her inner journey and how different she feels from the woman who first stepped onto this new trail to journey up the mountain. Woman is stronger, quieter within, more resilient, more in tune with her inner world than ever before. Her most recent journey took her to the stars and showed her the way of her destiny, to encourage and empower others, by being empowered within herself.

Woman is sitting in a clearing by the side of her path, her trail through life, taking some time to simply reflect on her own self-awareness. It has been quite a journey so far. She closes her eyes and her senses are sharpened without the visual cues that come with everyday vision. Woman hears the sounds of the birds winging their way overhead, and the rustle of the breeze through the treetops. She breathes in the aroma of nature, deep and pungent; she feels the earth beneath her. Her inner vision is beginning to show her a new step on this life path. Woman feels the heartbeat of the earth beneath her, a steady beat in tune with her own heart.

'Open your eyes,' she hears. As she does, she sees a man of indigenous appearance standing opposite her. In his hand he holds a large clear quartz crystal. Smaller ones lay on the earth around his feet. 'You have travelled well along this path,' he says, 'however, to journey along the next part of this trail, you require some new conductors of energy to align your crystalline body with that of the earth beneath you, and you require conductors of energy to connect you to the stars.'

Woman sits silently for a few moments, waiting, wondering what comes next. 'I am a Keeper of the Crystal and like many others throughout the Universe, it is my job to place new crystals within your etheric body to assist you to see with more clarity. To hear beyond the ordinary word. To feel your way with more understanding. To see and feel the portals of energy as you walk your path to higher wisdom.'

Woman stands and the man places the largest crystal within her heart space. He then places the smaller crystals in her throat and other significant areas within her etheric body.

The Keeper of the Crystal explains, 'These sacred crystals are activated as you move forward, acting as crystal guides for your journey. They amplify your energy fields creating a sensitivity to the earth's crystalline grids. The next part of your journey is to understand how to bring healing to the earth and your part in this greater journey.'

Woman closes her eyes again for a moment to feel the presence of the new crystals as they integrate into every part of her. When she opens her eyes once more, the Keeper of the Crystal is no longer with her, but she feels his words deep inside. The next part of her journey has begun.

MESSAGE

Activate the next part of your journey. Look after yourself. In order to live life at an optimal level, you need to look after mind, body, and soul. Everyone needs some recalibration from time to time. This time is one of soul-nourishing self exploration. Connect with the Goddess, the Earth Mother as you walk in nature. Connect with the stars as you lie under a star-filled dark night. You are aligning with a higher vibration now. Take some time just for you. The next part of your journey will require you to honour this sacred gift of time out.

CHAPTER 20

Honour your Journey

WOMAN WALKS HER trail, taking with her new knowledge, wisdom, and healing. She feels she has purpose to her direction. She notices that the climb is becoming steeper. Not harder, just steeper and it takes more effort and concentration now to keep moving forward up her mountain, one step at a time. The trail has also become narrower, keeping her focused on where she lands her feet. She is so intent on making it to the top of her mountain that she forgets to look around her.

Woman is looking at the ground, leaning forward, focused, determined, telling herself that she must reach the top of the mountain in the shortest amount of time. After all, she has learned a lot about herself on this new path, hasn't she?

Puffing a little from the exertion, she doesn't allow herself to have a break, even though she is the only one pushing herself. As she strides along, Woman eventually sees a pair of feet facing her in the middle of her trail. Woman has no alternative but to stop and look up. She gazes into the smiling face of one of the Ancient Ones. Surprised, Woman wonders what is coming next?

She steadies herself and places her backpack of sacred tools on the ground at her feet. The Ancient One gestures with her arm at the magnificent view around them. With a quick intake of breath, Woman sees the vista around her. She realises that she has been so focused on where to place her feet and her destination that she forgot to look around her. She didn't look at how far she has already journeyed. Instead, Woman is focused on how far she has to go and the steepness of the climb.

Woman hears in her heart and mind, 'It is time to stop and look at the view around you. Soon it will be the dark of the moon time just before the new moon begins to illuminate your path. Stop and honour the earth, honour the directions, honour Grandmother Moon and Grandfather Sun. Honour Mother Earth. Honour the Goddess within.'

'Take out your sacred tools, particularly your drum and as the sun sets and day becomes an all-embracing darkness, beat in time to the heartbeat of Mother Earth. Allow yourself to simply be in this space and allow the messages to come to you at this potent time. I will sit with you and hold this sacred space for you.'

Woman sits on the earth exactly where she is and opens her backpack, pulling out her drum. Closing her eyes, she begins to beat a rhythmic beat, creating a spontaneous ceremony. The Ancient One holds the sacred space and chants. The energy of the moment is building.

Woman knows a new message is coming to her now. She opens her heart and her mind to allow it to come to her on the light of love. Woman's lesson is to know when to stop, to take a break and when to honour the cycles of life and simply be open to something new. The way she was going, she would have missed the beauty of her surroundings and the inherent messages. Woman had not realised that she had already journeyed one full cycle. Woman holds no expectations, just the joyful feeling of magic with the coming of an all-embracing darkness and a star-filled sky.

MESSAGE

The unexpected will come to you. Your heart space will require spontaneity as you honour the gift of knowing what needs to be done and just doing it. Do something sacred and be spontaneous in the moment. This is sure to open a new door of possibility.

CHAPTER 21

Sanctuary

WOMAN IS MORE aware of her surroundings now. Her impromptu ceremony on the dark of the moon opened her heart to the warm inner beauty of her world. She has learned the lesson of knowing when to stop and journey within. She has learned the lesson of looking around her at the beauty of life, rather than at her feet. In the light of a new day, as the sun rises, Woman is already walking mindfully, watching, drinking in the world around her with love. Her heart is full.

As she walks, Woman feels a stirring in the air. The energy around her is shifting. All of her senses are on high alert. She slows her pace. The sky quickly darkens; clouds are building, shutting out the sunlight. The wind begins to blow, almost sweeping her feet from under her. Thunder claps loudly, beating a rhythmic and steady beat. Lightning begins to strike the ground around her, offering an almost negatively charged perspective on her surroundings. Rain beats down and pelts Woman with large drops of cold water, drenching her instantly.

Shivering with cold, Woman looks for a place to take refuge. She sees a small opening in the rocks beside her trail. She ducks into the opening hoping there is nothing untoward waiting for her. It is a small cave and it will do for now as it is dry and warm, keeping her safe from the elements outside.

She notices a candle and some matches just beside the entrance of the cave. Gathering them up, Woman strikes the match and lights the candle wondering how it has come to be in this small respite space along her own trail. Turning to face the inside of the cave, Woman is surprised to see a fireplace in the centre, surrounded by stones and set with wood, ready to light. A magnificent deep violet velvet robe is laid out nearby on a beautifully carved stone bench. Woman wonders if she dares light the fire and don the robe. She is feeling cold to the bone from the sudden storm which she can hear is still raging outside the cave, and her clothes are wet through.

She hears the word 'trust' in her heart and mind. Woman closes her eyes for a moment to feel the right thing to do. She wants to be warm and dry, but she doesn't know if the occupant of the cave might soon return and she has no idea what the outcome might be. So, trust is the key to warmth or to return to the storm raging outside the door.

Within her heart and mind, she hears, 'It is important to take refuge from life's storms. It is important to see what is right in front of you that will offer you nurturance, warmth, and comfort. *This* cave exists within you. It is your sanctuary when life throws you a storm. You do not always have to walk in the storm. It is perfectly fine to retreat until it passes. Not all storms are there to be weathered.'

'*This* is your lesson. *This*, is discernment.'

Woman knows now that retreating with a purpose offers precious time to regroup and build energy to keep the trails of life moving with love. She knows that she cannot always keep moving forward. There are times to move and times to retreat is a mantra to keep close to her now on her journey. Woman has a backpack of sacred tools for the journey and lessons she is learning along the way, and now, Woman is also living by the wise words offered through her heart. Smiling to herself, Woman takes her matches and strikes them, lighting the fire within. It is right to do so.

MESSAGE

Sometimes you need to retreat and take shelter while the storms of life rage outside of you. It's okay to give yourself permission to withdraw for a while. Sometimes you need the comfort of what this retreat offers in order to know when to be still and nourish yourself and when to return to the world and your journey, your trail. Now is a time to retreat into your inner cave to nourish something within you that has been battling a storm outside of your control. It will pass soon enough when you look after you. There is a time for retreat and a time for advancing. Both require your intuitive input.

CHAPTER 22

It's All about Love

THE STORM HAS passed and Woman emerges from her sanctuary into the bright light of day. The sky is a vibrant blue, the sun is warm on her skin. Her surroundings are fresh and clean. She feels content in her understanding that it is perfectly fine to retreat for a while in the face of an intense storm.

Woman sits on the earth in the middle of her path while she considers her next step. She feels it is time to just be, to walk mindfully, to stop and smell the flowers and breathe in the pure mountain air. A time to listen to the birds winging their way overhead and observe the signs nature offers her.

First though, Woman opens her backpack of sacred tools for the journey. She takes out her cards with sacred symbols drawn on them. They reflect the symbols on the floor of the cave she visited. The same cave where she received her sacred tools. It seems so long ago.

Shuffling the deck, she clears her mind. She has no need for a specific answer to a question. She just feels the need to open her heart and mind to what the symbols mean to her personally.

Woman's breathing slows to a meditative pace. Her mind is clear. Her heart is open and full of love. Shuffling the cards without thought was never easy in the past. Her mind was always busy and yet now, in this moment, Woman is fully present to where she is and who she is in her sacred womanliness. One card flies out of the deck and lands on her lap. One symbol, and a clear message for her journey. A heart. Be love. Always, *be* love, and you will attract love to you. A simple, succinct message.

Woman returns her cards to her backpack of sacred tools and stands to look around her. Her heart *is* full of love. Woman looks skyward and sees one white cloud, in the shape of a heart. She looks to the path beneath her feet and a rock, in the shape of a heart is in front of her. A plant at the edge of her path has heart-shaped leaves.

Woman sighs in contentment. She knows now that the lesson is to be open to the symbols of life that are everywhere. You just need to be willing to see them, not only with your eyes but also with your heart. Understanding of the symbols comes when you notice the repetitive signs offered. Woman dons her backpack and begins to walk her trail once more. Love is all around her.

MESSAGE

Love is here to claim your heart. There is a need to feel and express love, for yourself, for others, for your environment, for life. When you open to the love that is you, life offers a smile, an embrace, a new beginning. Be love now, always be love. Life is about to shine for you with a vibrancy not seen in a while.

CHAPTER 23

Keep Going

WOMAN HAS BEEN walking up this trail on her personal mountain for a while now and there have been many lessons and many revelations on her journey. Most of all, Woman is learning how to open her heart to love.

The sun is warm on her face, the light breeze is playing with her hair. The sounds of the birds, particularly the eagle is music to her ears. Woman's heart is full.

Today, she feels, is the first day of the rest of her life. Her backpack is light. Her footfalls are strong and determined. Woman raises her face to the sun and then looks around at the vista surrounding her. She looks further, to the other mountains, in a mountain range that seems to go on forever. She can see the mountains close to her. She can see other women walking their trails.

Woman stops and closes her eyes. With her inner vision, she sees that women walking their path are at different stages on their journey. She can see that some are just beginning their journey while others are walking with their heads down and not seeing what is around them. Woman recognises her own journey within these inner visions and can see how far she has travelled.

She continues to look inward and can see some of the women are smiling and in a similar position to her. Others are much higher on their trail. Some have reached the pinnacle of their mountain and are resting as they take in the whole vista.

Woman smiles to herself as she has just learned the lesson that people journey at different rates on their chosen trails. They walk and grow into their journey at a different pace to others, and that is the way it is supposed to be.

All of these trails, on all of these mountains, lead towards the top of their particular mountain. All trails walk side by side and link together, and one woman will encourage those beside her, and so on.

Woman looks to the mountains beside her once more. She smiles with encouragement. 'Keep going,' she whispers. 'Look up not down.' The women on their own trails smile back and whisper on the breezes, 'thank you, I needed that love and encouragement.'

Woman is ready for her next adventure and continues her journey upward, her footfalls light upon her trail as she ascends towards a much bigger and expansive view of life.

MESSAGE

Never give up. Your journey is unique to you, and all those around you will walk at their own pace. Encourage those who share your life to see the beautiful vista around them. This is a time to lead by example. There is a much bigger view to see and more unique trails to follow. You are being offered an opportunity now to be more than you think you are capable of being.

CHAPTER 24

The Child Within

THE SUN IS shining on Woman's face. The path has widened. Her backpack is light. She feels soul-nourished on this journey. Woman has been walking up her mountain for some time and the terrain has been easy going for a while.

Woman stops. She hears a sound. Quiet sobbing. It is coming from the direction of the bushes beside her trail. Woman wonders how anyone could be sad on such a beautiful day. She wants to keep moving with the beauty of what is around her, but she cannot ignore the plight of someone crying. Someone yet to be identified on her trail.

Woman makes her way through the bushes and into a small clearing. There is a child sitting in the clearing.

She is grubby and thin. Tears are streaking down her small face from big eyes as blue as the sky above.

Woman gently sits down beside her and lays her backpack on the ground, careful not to scare the young child. Woman guesses her age to be around 10 years old. 'Why are you crying?' she asks the child. The child turns her head towards Woman and Woman is once more struck by the blueness of her eyes. There is something about those eyes that she cannot fathom. The child doesn't answer with words. Instead, she places her hand over her heart and the tears begin to flow again.

Woman wonders silently why this child is on *her* trail and why she feels a sudden wrenching within her own heart. It must be the distress of this small, ragged child that is touching her so deeply.

'No,' she hears in her own heart and mind. 'I am the child within you.' I am here to help you heal the ancient wounds you hold within. You have journeyed a long way on these trails through life and it is time to bring healing home to your inner child.

Woman is quiet. She understands now that she has ignored this inner child for so long. She realises just how much she has missed the child within. Woman knows now that this child is ragged and thin and distraught because she has not been nourished for many years.

'How can I change this?' Woman asks. 'Is it too late to help us both?'

'It is never too late to heal ancient wounds,' she hears. 'What do I need to do?' she asks. 'Put your arms around me,' the child tells her, 'and love me.'

'Is it really as simple as that?' Woman asks. 'Yes,' she is told. 'Hold me close to you.'

Woman picks up the child and places her on her lap, wrapping her arms around her in a loving embrace. Closing her eyes, Woman feels the love she has for this child, that is a part of her, fill her to overflowing. She feels the ancient wounds buried deep within her rise the surface and float away. As each hurt leaves, she feels lighter than ever before.

The healing is done. Opening her eyes Woman sees a light around her. The child has transformed into an Angel. Her vibrant blue eyes are shining with love.

'You have healed the ancient wounds of the past,' Woman hears. 'Through your nourishing embrace we are now one once more. Remember, as you journey now, to love with the innocence of a child. Remember to play and to laugh. Remember to speak honestly. Remember me and that all healing takes place within love. I am always around you and within you. Remember me, remember us.'

Woman feels only the love of this healing experience and sits comfortably within the silence of this love. She rests for a while before she continues on with the next part of her journey.

MESSAGE

It is never too late to access your inner child. She is always with you, and yet so often, we deny her a voice in this adult world. She needs to know she is safe now, that she is loved and acknowledged. Today remember to laugh and play and be the joy of the innocent child. It is in the love that comes from the joy and laughter that old wounds can heal.

CHAPTER 25

Twin Hearts

WOMAN HAS CLIMBED many mountains in her life and each one has brought challenges, learning and love and this one is no different. She loves this journey and how much it is opening her eyes and her heart. Her deeply feminine spirit has never felt more alive. She has never felt lighter or fitter than right at this moment.

Woman looks to the top of the mountain. She is getting closer now and she feels the shift in her personal vibration, but there is an edginess creeping in now. A need to revisit a part of her she has denied for a long time. She can feel the masculine calling to her, through her heart.

Woman slows her pace, wanting to take her time to think about all the different scenarios this might bring up for her. She knows she has learned how to self-love. She knows she has healed her inner child, but this one feels like a test of wills. Who will win the battle she whispers to herself.

Woman focuses on the sound of her breath. She can hear her own heartbeat in her ears. She feels that her guides have deserted her at this crucial time. Woman feels completely alone. She hears in her heart and mind, 'You know you are never truly alone. We are always here with you.' Woman is immediately apologetic, knowing they are truly there but sometimes the path just needs to be journeyed to see what lies in front of her.

Woman walks silently now, mindful of her footfalls. Her heart is still beating loudly, like the rhythm of a big bass drum. She looks directly ahead of her, and around her, waiting, waiting for what is coming to her now.

A narrow track leads off her main trail, and she knows it is hers to take if she chooses. Or, she can keep walking. She hears in her heart and mind, 'It's time to heal the wounds of all relationships, past, present, and future.'

Knowing her guides are correct, Woman sighs and pushes her shoulders back and takes the narrow path. It leads to another clearing. There is a bright and beautiful rug spread on the ground and a candelabra with large pillar candles burning in their holders, creating a seductive scene.

Woman shrugs off her backpack and sits on the rug. She has to admit it feels beautiful here, there is so much peace. Woman closes her eyes for a few moments and breathes in the intoxicating aromas of her surroundings.

She feels him close now, but her eyes remain closed. Someone sits down opposite her on the rug. She slowly opens her eyes and allows the man opposite her to take her hands gently in his. 'We have been apart a long time you and I,' he says. Woman can only nod in agreement. She is fearful of her voice betraying her emotions for the moment.

'It is time for us to become as one once more, to become whole again, to heal the old wounds that separated us for so long,' she hears. Woman knows this is true, however she has denied this part of her for most of her life. She has denied that she is indeed a blend of the feminine and the masculine. There has been a great deal of pain in her life, so she pushed this very powerful part of herself away a long time ago.

Woman closes her eyes and sits quietly. She asks her guides for help. They reply, 'To become whole one must embrace both aspects of self. Both parts are equal and in order to operate at an optimum in a given life, one needs the other to function in wholeness. Both aspects have their vulnerabilities and their strengths and help each other navigate life's journey.' This makes a lot of sense to Woman. She feels its truth in her heart.

She opens her eyes and says, 'I am ready to become whole again. I know I have a fabulous journey ahead of me. I need you just as much as you need me.'

Woman's guides surround her and her masculine counterpart. They ask them to place a hand on each other's heart. Warm, vibrant energy begins to circulate around their arms and through their respective hearts. The warmth increases its momentum until Woman feels it turn to love. Faster and faster the energy spins until everything around them disappears, and it is just the two of them, hand to heart, heart to hand until a crescendo is reached.

Suddenly everything stops and the clearing is once more around her. She smiles to herself. She and the masculine have united in sacred sex. Twin hearts now beat as one. She is whole once more. There is more love within her now than she ever thought possible. So this is wholeness, she thinks. This is the way it is supposed to be. 'Yes,' she hears her masculine whisper from deep within her. 'This *is* how it is supposed to be my love.' Woman is content as she sleeps now, wrapped in the arms of peace and love, her guides watching over her. Balance is restored.

MESSAGE

The need for balance is urgent in a world out of balance between the feminine and masculine. It is time for you to embrace that balance as you marry the two halves of the same whole. You will be asked to help bring balance to a situation, to see two sides of the same metaphorical coin.

CHAPTER 26

Birth

WOMAN VIEWS HER world with fresh eyes. She is aware that she can see more than ever before. Not just with her eyes but with her inner vision, her inner senses. Woman takes a breath because she is witnessing the birth of a new cycle. It is sunrise and Woman feels content now as with the rising sun, new awareness, new birth and new opportunities are being created. She can feel them, know them with her mind and her heart.

Woman ponders her recent journeys. She has healed her inner child. She has merged with the masculine, her other half, her masculine reflection in an act of sacred sex through heart connection and now, she is ready to birth herself into a new adventure.

Woman has been walking and experiencing this powerful and ever-changing journey for some time, and she is feeling clear in her mind and in her heart. Something is stirring deep within her. She feels it within her creative centre, her womb, her sacral. Ideas are forming. A knowing of the next step, when she emerges from this intense journey, is growing within her. Everything she is learning about herself on this mountain trail is what she will integrate into her everyday life.

Woman places a hand on her belly, feeling the stirrings of new life, new thoughts, feelings, and ideas. The energy of this profound moment is about knowing she has a greater purpose in life. She has come so far on her journey and on this mountain. This time in her life is teaching her so much, healing old wounds and is showing her the beauty of the world that exists beyond the ordinary.

Woman raises her face to the warmth and light of the rising sun, remembering her way. She remembers that she had a dream and now it is coming to a time where she will fulfil her destiny. She doesn't need to know exactly what that is, or where it will lead. All Woman needs to know, for now, is that she is growing new ideas within her. She is living her destiny simply by working with each lesson that comes her way and understanding those lessons. Once she has learned something powerful and positive about herself, it cannot be unlearned. What the rising sun has taught her, is that each new day is a blessing. An opportunity to birth the next part of her journey, with love.

MESSAGE

The rising sun gives birth to a new day, every day. Held within that sun are all the possibilities for the day ahead. Now is the time to bring forward your dreams, your ideas and give birth to them. You have earned this time of birth because of the trust you have placed on your journey. See something you have dreamed with fresh eyes.

CHAPTER 27

Worth

WOMAN IS BACK on her trail. New awakenings are stirring from deep within her, from deep within her sacred womb. She is getting close to the top of her mountain now, but she is aware that the journey takes as long as it takes and that there is likely to be more lessons and love to be experienced along the way.

She has only just had this thought when standing on her trail are three Ancient Ones. Women of a high order. She takes in their appearance. Ethereal but vibrant. Ancient faces. Magnificent rich-coloured robes. Spectacular sparkling crowns upon their heads. Tall, strong women, ancient and beautiful, surrounded by an aura of pure love. Woman can see it all, and she feels their presence in her own heart.

Woman catches her breath, taking a few moments to take it all in. The Ancient Ones are silent. They are watching, waiting. Woman begins to become anxious in the silence. Her mind is attempting to second guess why they are here, what they could possibly want with her. The silence continues. Woman becomes more anxious, thinking they are going to send her back to a point she perhaps hasn't dealt with properly, a lesson not learned, or even back to the beginning.

Woman feels insignificant in the presence of such power. The silence is deafening, her heartbeat is pounding in her ears, and anxiety is peaking. She cannot take much more. Her mind is in overdrive: thinking, worrying, sorting, trying to come up with a plausible reason for them to be standing on her trail. Still watching, waiting in silence.

Nothing has been spoken but Woman, in her anxiety, has told herself that her worthiness is in question, that she is not worthy of this journey. Woman feels hurt, sad. Anger begins to churn, even though nothing has been spoken. She turns around and takes three steps back down her trail, wanting to find her place, a lower position than here because she is not worthy of reaching for the summit. She must have missed a step, or worse, done something wrong. She knows it. Her beautiful expressions of love and joy have vanished.

Just as she is about to take another step, Woman hears, 'You are the creator of your own feelings of unworthiness. We stood in silence, in our own power and you did the rest. You do not yet feel your worthiness for your own power. This lesson is to believe in your worth, see your value, honour who *you* are, not as a measure of what you perceive are others' opinions, and keep going.'

Woman turns back to face the Ancient Ones. They are smiling, sending love to her on energetic light waves, healing her wounds of unworthiness. Woman was prepared to return to a lower vibration even though she had mastered the journey to get to this point. This is a tough lesson, to learn how to believe in herself and her journey, to see her value in the face of perceived challenges. The Ancient Ones are fading from her vision, leaving love, and power in their wake. The rest she knows, is up to her.

MESSAGE

Stand in your own power. Feel your worth. You have more to offer life than perhaps you are aware. There is a challenge coming. Will you return to your old ways of being or stand strong in your worth?

CHAPTER 28

Laughter

WOMAN HAS EXPERIENCED a harsh lesson as she unravelled her worthiness in the face of power she thought was greater than hers. The lesson is well learned and timely as she journeys toward the pinnacle of her personal mountain along a trail filled with lessons, challenges as well as joy and understanding about her own self.

It's not far now, she thinks. However, she also knows that before she reaches the top of this mountain, there will be more lessons and understanding about her journey.

Woman's heart and mind are wide open to the potential, joy and opportunities that are ahead of her. She feels it with every part of her, and she is ready for the next step on life's trail.

Woman's vision is opening further with every footfall she takes. She sees flashes of light at every turn, flickers of different colours darting around her, bumping into her. The higher she journeys, the more she is becoming aware of these lights and she wonders what they could be. They must be something sacred, she thinks.

One of her many guides appears, a woman of indeterminate age who walks beside her. She appears strong, round, with twinkling blue eyes. She keeps pace with Woman effortlessly. Unsure whether she should just keep walking or stop and speak with her guide to find out what the lesson is this time, Woman decides to smile at her guide and keep walking. She is sure she will know soon enough what is required of her. She feels more powerful in herself now after that last lesson.

They walk together for a time in the quiet and the coloured lights are darting all around them both. So many more of them now. Woman finally asks her guide about the lights she can see everywhere and asks what they are. She can't stand not knowing any longer.

Her guide chuckles and says, 'I have been waiting for you to ask a question.'

'Why did I have to ask?' Woman says, 'Why not just tell me what I need to know?'

'That wouldn't be much fun now would it?' Her guide declares, eyes twinkling just that bit brighter with mischief. It appears this guide of Woman's has a sense of humour. 'We all do,' she hears. 'You humans can be so serious when it comes to learning. It's time to lighten up and laugh.'

Woman harrumphs, then clears her throat and apologises, which sends her guide into fits of belly laughter. 'You can't help yourself, can you? You think everything to be learned in life needs reverence. What if I told you that the sacredness of life is best learned with laughter, particularly at self?'

Woman stops and stands with her mouth open. Did her guide just tell her she is stiff and has no sense of humour? This is apparently very funny to her guide who now rocks and roars with laughter.

'Lighten up, laugh,' she hears. The lights are bumping into her and she feels a presence within each little spark. Each time they bump into her, she hears an infectious giggle. Woman begins to laugh with her guide and with the lights which are now creating a whirlwind of energy around her.

The more she laughs, the more her vision opens. Woman can see faeries, elementals, cheeky sprites, strange owls and many others she doesn't know. They are playing with her, bringing joy to her soul. Their fun is offering her a much-needed lesson. Make time to laugh at life's journey. Life lessons are not always harsh or difficult. Many lessons just involve an injection of much-needed fun. What a journey. Who knew, Woman thinks, that a lesson could bring such immense joy to the journey.

MESSAGE

Have you been too serious lately? It's time to laugh out loud, to have some fun. Life is not meant to be taken so seriously all the time. Laughing at self will open your inner visions, your feelings. Laughter has a way of raising the vibration in a room so that solutions to perceived issues can be found with ease. Lighten the mood. Try it!

CHAPTER 29

Be a Leader

WOMAN IS STILL giggling as she continues along her trail. She shakes her head in wonder that her thoughts always appeared to be serious on her journey. She understands now that laughter will often help her learn her lessons in a profound way. She is more likely to remember lessons learned with love and laughter.

Woman's thoughts drift to family and friends, her tribe. She has been so caught up in her own journey, she feels she has neglected those around her a little. Her heart aches to be close to her loved ones. The choices she has made in life have not always been conducive to supporting relationships and yet, now that she has taken the road less travelled and learned a great deal about herself, she feels almost ready to return to her everyday world.

Woman knows that to live a fulfilled life, it comes with many different people and experiences that will test her journey, that will allow her to grow within the context of relationships of all kinds. She understands that the tests will come to her, to see just how much she has learned on this journey, this trail. She wonders how she may be a guide to others, to those she loves. She wonders how she can encourage them to walk their own trails of understanding.

As soon as these thoughts pop into her mind, her family and soul tribe are standing in front of her. Woman stops in her tracks and stares at the people facing her. Silently, they turn and face away from her and Woman wonders what she has done to deserve their turning away.

They begin to walk away from the trail and into a clearing. Woman follows. In the centre is a large, central fire which is blazing with orange, red and yellow flames. Each member of the group walks silently around the circle and takes a place beside the fire. Woman finds a place which has been left for her. She shrugs off her backpack of sacred tools and places it on the ground beside her and waits to see what will be her lesson on this day.

One of the elders in the group speaks to her. Woman exhales sharply. She realises that she has been holding her breath, waiting for someone to speak. 'We are the higher self aspect of your tribe. We are here to remind you that we all have our own journeys to take. You do not need to do anything to influence our journey. We have our own soul agreement to fulfil,' she hears. He falls silent.

Another tribe member speaks. 'You are fulfilling your own journey and as such, you are a leader. However, it is your journey to lead by example. When one of us is ready to hear your words, learn from you, or listen to your stories we will seek you out because this is our journey.' Silence now.

A third member speaks. 'Our higher selves know your journey and what it has taken for you to arrive at this point. However, while we congratulate you, we need to journey at our own pace. Some here are walking with you already. Some are walking behind you as you light the way and others are ahead of you, lighting the way forward for you. So, you see, we all have our journey to navigate at our own pace. Love will always bind us through our tribe connection but being a master, is personal. We are family. Remember that.'

Woman absorbs all she has heard as they sit now in warm, comfortable silence around the sacred fire. She has a great deal to contemplate. Her lesson is to understand that everyone has their own sacred journey to follow. She can only live her life according to her own experiences, as will others. Some will seek her for those experiences and others will discover a different way, and all ways will be right for that person.

Woman sees that to live your life to the best of your own ability is to lead that life by example. When some of your tribe are ready, they will want to know more about the journey. This is her understanding. Her tribe fades from view, but she sits there a little longer, warmed by the sacred fire, loving imprints filling the space as she integrates her lessons, before she moves forward on the next part of her journey. Her heart is full of love and new awareness.

MESSAGE

Those who are a part of your tribe are on their own journey. You may not agree with some of the choices made by them, however it *is* their journey to take. You are the leader who leads her tribe by example. Sowing the seeds of the way will gain the best outcomes. Someone will seek your wise counsel. Listen and share your story.

CHAPTER 30

The Saboteur

WOMAN HAS SHOULDERED her backpack ready to walk her trail once more. She knows her backpack is full of sacred tools and yet she hasn't felt the need to work with them a great deal on this journey. There is a lifetime ahead and perhaps more, to work with them. She has been carrying this backpack of tools almost without thought, certain that at some stage she will need them. Surely, we must need to work with our sacred tools on this journey through life, she asks herself.

'I am glad you asked that,' she hears. Woman spins around on the spot, however she cannot see anyone. 'Down here.' Woman looks down and sees a small creature of indeterminate species. 'What do you want?' Woman asks.

'Look,' the creature says, 'I'm here to offer you some sound advice. You have journeyed up this mountain, and you have learned so many lessons. It's an uphill journey and yes, sure you are not far away from the top now, but really, wouldn't you like to stop now?'

'I need to keep going,' Woman tells him, 'I have come this far, I do need to keep going.'

'Who says you do? Those silly old women who bring you challenges on this *trail* they call life? Pfftt. You don't have to do anything you don't want to. Cross my heart and hope to die,' he tells her.

Woman wavers. She *is* rather tired, she thinks. She was full of vibrancy not long ago, but now the creature has highlighted it, she decides that she does need a rest. She deserves a rest. Woman sits on the earth and shrugs off her backpack. What do I need these tools for anyway, she grumpily asks herself? Woman's high vibration has slipped and her mood is shaping her journey now. 'That's right,' the little creature tells her. 'You don't need any of this. Why don't you head on home? You don't need to reach the top of this mountain. You have worked hard enough already. You've done enough.'

Woman stands and begins to walk back down the mountain again. Instead of feeling lighter though, Woman feels heavier as she walks. This can't be right, she thinks. If

I have done enough, as the little creature says, and I have dispensed with the backpack of sacred tools, then I should feel light and happy.

Woman stops walking back down the mountain and takes stock of the situation. She was happy with her journey, walking towards the pinnacle of her mountain. Even though she only worked with her backpack of sacred tools intermittently, they were hers to do with as she wished. She felt light on her journey. Then this little creature appears and plants thoughts that were not even on her radar.

Woman recognises now exactly who this creature is. She turns and walks back up to where he is still standing with a big smirk on his face. '*You*, are the saboteur and you have come to me to try and halt my journey. I know you. I recognise you and how you work. You try and undermine me when life is going along nicely. Well, not this time! Get away from me and my sacred tools.'

The saboteur has been identified, and he knows he cannot stay now he has been called out. He turns and huffs away until he is no longer visible to Woman. Woman has been tested by this creature many times over her lifetime. He has appeared to her under many guises. She is so close to achieving her goal, but she almost let his low vibration stop her from reaching the top of the mountain. It almost stopped her from working with her own sacred tools. Woman has learned many things on her journey, and now, when she is again being tested by lower vibrations, she is quicker to recognise and release them and keep moving forward.

Woman shoulders her backpack once more and with determination and lightness of step, she continues on her journey up her personal mountain of self-discovery.

MESSAGE

The saboteur will come when you least expect it and try to pull you off course. He is quite comfortable with chaos and this new energy of reaching for the pinnacle is something he is not comfortable with. You will be tested along your journey. Challenge this saboteur and journey onward with love for the adventure.

CHAPTER 31

Stay Focused on the Present

WOMAN HAS KEPT her feet firmly on the trail, taking detours where necessary but generally speaking, she has stayed grounded. She is walking mindfully, looking up and around her, not down. Woman is aware that this part of her journey will soon be over, and another adventure awaits her.

Her mind begins to wander to her future potential. A future she knows includes being a better healer. Woman's thoughts are drifting to the knowledge that a healer can only take others where she herself has been on her own journey. Woman is feeling quite pleased with this potential future. Her thoughts are so focused on the possibilities of what is to come, that she is no longer mindful of where she is placing her feet. Woman stumbles and falls flat on her face. Her knees are torn and bleeding, her body jarred from the fall. Nothing appears to be broken except her pride.

She looks behind her to see what tripped her up. A small crystal is sticking up out of the ground in the middle of her trail. 'How can something so small trip me up?' Woman wonders. She crawls back to the crystal and attempts to pick it up to examine it. It won't budge. It's stuck firmly in the ground.

Woman forgets her bumps and scrapes and finds a stick nearby and begins to dig around the crystal. She thinks it must be meant for her to add to her backpack of sacred tools. Woman digs and digs, but the more she digs, the more of the crystal there is below the surface. Woman widens her dig area, curious now about just how big this crystal is, and just how deep it is buried in the earth. Her wounds forgotten, she is on a quest to know about this crystal that tripped her up.

No guides come to her. She is on her own with this one. Woman is aware that this time she must find her own answers, understand the lesson herself.

The crystal is rose quartz, the stone of unconditional love. A stone of love tripped her up with just the smallest tip. Woman continues to dig. The hole is getting larger. The crystal is deeper and much bigger than she imagined when she saw what her stumbling block was.

Finally, Woman sits back on her haunches. This crystal is not going to be moved she thinks. It is too big and too deep. It seems it would be better to let it remain in the earth. If it is not for her to add to her sacred tools, why then did that one small piece trip her up? What is the lesson here? Woman gets up off the ground and begins to walk around the crystal. She opens her awareness, her inner vision, to see beyond the ordinary. This is a lesson for her to learn, without input from her guides. Woman breathes deeply and continues to circle the crystal. As she walks, she watches the crystal. She realises that she can communicate with it. Not only that, the tip she tripped over on this trail is glowing brighter than any other part of the crystal.

In her heart and her mind Woman hears, 'If your mind journeys too far into the future, something small and seemingly insignificant will often trip you up. When you attempt to dig deeper though, you see just how big the story, the lesson, or the life journey truly is and that can overwhelm you long before you are ready to see the whole picture. You really only need to deal with what is being shown to you at a given time. If the rest is meant for you to discover, more will be uncovered in due time.'

Woman sits back and digests this information and how well it sits with her. The lesson is to work with what you know and see to begin with, what is obvious, while knowing there is more to uncover, more to know. When what is buried is ready to be known, it *will* become known to you. Don't become distracted and dig a hole to try to dislodge it before it is ready to be revealed. Trying to work with the whole picture at once is hard work and can become overwhelming and time-consuming if you try to push it. Nobody knows the depth of the story or journey being uncovered. Each time something is to be revealed, it will become apparent and even trip you up if necessary. Spending too much time digging can take you away from your greater purpose in life. Everything is in its right timing. Heal and understand what is presenting itself now. It is a part of Woman's journey to know this, to be a better healer. To work with what is tripping someone up will help the stories buried deep within heal.

Woman covers the crystal once more, knowing that all the time spent uncovering the depth of the crystal made no difference as she had initially ignored the piece wanting to be noticed. She was digging deep when it wasn't necessary. Who knows how big and how old it is? Yes, a better healer will see what others need them to see, but she will know there is so much more to the story that will present itself at the right time. Love is the key. Woman is content; she is mindful of her footsteps in the present moment once more.

MESSAGE

What is on the surface is the beginning but not the end of a story and yet, it is the place to begin a healing journey. Once a story has begun to present itself, in time more of it will be revealed. For now, be aware of a story beginning to emerge into your conscious thoughts. Stay present and work with what you know. As you start the journey the next piece of the story will be uncovered, with love. All at the right time.

CHAPTER 32

Matriarchal Support

WOMAN CAN SEE the top now, the pinnacle of this sacred mountain. Her journey is nearly over. Excitement begins to build within her. There is a part of her that feels trepidation over the completion of this journey. What lies beyond this mountain, she wonders?

Woman rounds a gentle bend in her trail. Women line the sides of her trail, forming a guard of honour. She looks into the faces of the women closest to her. She recognises the faces of her loved ones, her matrilineal line, her ancestors, the Ancient Ones who walked this trail long before her.

Tears spring to her eyes as she begins to walk between the two rows of women. The women reach out to her, and each time Woman feels their touch on her arm, she feels their love surge through her. She feels their strength, their courage, their determination. She also feels the harshness of what they endured in their lifetimes and how they survived and thrived. All of this information comes from a single touch and she knows their story.

One of Woman's ancestors steps forward and stands before her. She reaches out a hand to take Woman's and lead her forward. Woman hears, 'This is your time now. You have almost reached the top of this mountain journey. What you do now is up to you. Leave a legacy for those who walk the trails behind you. It doesn't matter what you do, as long as you do it with love.'

Woman's ancestor steps back with the other women. Another steps forward. Woman hears, 'We can only lead where we have journeyed ourselves in life. When someone is ready to hear you, they will come to you. You will hear their stories and know them from your own experiences.' The ancestor steps back as another takes her place. 'Be gentle and compassionate with yourself first. You cannot offer others wisdom for their journey if you first do not look after yourself. Self-nourishment is important to the journey ahead.'

Once more an ancestor steps forward. 'What I need to share with you is important to your journey ahead. You do not have all of the answers for all of the people who come to you for your wise words. Sometimes, all you need to do is listen. Remember these words in the years ahead.'

The women are silent now. Smiling with love at Woman, wishing her well on her last steps of this journey up the mountain and beyond into a new journey. Woman looks back down the trail at her ancestors. Her heart is full of love and wonder at what lies ahead. She turns back up the mountain and walks forward, knowing her matrilineal line will always be with her on her journey.

MESSAGE

Knowing you always have the love and support of your matrilineal line is important to the journey. They paved the way so that you may be where you are right now, so that you may learn from their journeying. You don't need to know the answers to everything at this time. This may be a time to just listen. A smile, a hug, a listening ear is often all that is required on someone's journey. You may need someone to listen to your story right now. You will know who will listen, with love.

CHAPTER 33

The Pinnacle

THE FINAL TURN and Woman steps onto the top of her mountain, her quest complete. Emotions threaten to swamp her. She's done it. She has reached the summit, the pinnacle, the top. Woman is not sure how she should feel. Happy? Free? A little lost now this particular journey is over?

Woman looks around her, at the mountain range that extends as far as the eye can see in any direction. The mountains are different heights, linked together at their base, one to the next. Woman can again see her connection to the other women climbing their own personal mountains.

She sees the top of her personal mountain as a journey to be celebrated and yet she feels alone. There is no-one around her to celebrate her journey. Woman is bemused by her feelings. Why did she climb this mountain? Why did she undertake this journey with all of its twists and turns and lessons if there is no-one to share the stories with?

There is so much beauty around her from this vantage point and yet she feels very alone. Tears begin to flow. Her heart is breaking at what she considers loss of her loved ones. They have abandoned her while she journeyed this path. Well they have, haven't they?

Woman gazes out at the world around her, at the other mountains. She looks down at the trail she has journeyed, and in her eyes, it looks very ordinary now. How could she have thought it was special, this trail?

She shakes herself out of her reverie, puts her shoulders back, head up and breathes in the majesty around her. I am Woman, she thinks, and this journey was worthy of me. I am strong. I have purpose now. I am ready for the next adventure. Those who want to hear my stories will find me.

Just as Woman is about to journey back down her mountain, she notices movement in the bushes beside her. She begins to hear chanting and singing, drumming and laughter.

She steps through the bushes into a clearing and sees people having fun. There is a table laden with food and wine. Women and men are dancing. Some she recognises as her friends and family. Some are her guides. Everyone is here together as one unified group. Vibrant colours are a feast to her eyes. A fire is blazing and the smell of the food is tantalising. An Ancient Woman holding a staff ambles to her side. 'What is this?' Woman asks.

The Ancient One replies, 'This is your tribe. You still have the jungles to explore, deep caves within the earth to seek, other mountains to climb and the depths of the ocean to swim. Each journey is a success, a victory to be celebrated and for now, dear beautiful Woman, we come together to celebrate you and your journey. Come now and join in your celebration.'

The Ancient One steps forward and just as Woman steps to join her, she has a knowing that as one journey ends, another is just beginning. Each journey undertaken is a powerful celebration of life. Smiling, Woman begins to dance.

MESSAGE

Dance in celebration of a journey completed. There is a new journey waiting for you to explore and a new trail to follow, however for now, this is your time to be celebrated. You followed the trails well and now you will take what you have learned about yourself into your everyday world, with love. Those who love you support your journey. Believe in you!

Jude Downes is a story-weaver of metaphoric stories for journeying and healing. She is a Clairvoyant Medium and an Intuitive Mentor with certificates in Psycho Spiritual Hypnotherapy, Colour Therapy and Reiki. Jude's healing words work with metaphors through the power of story to affect deep and lasting transformation. She is passionate about helping others on their life journey. Jude is a 'Healer with Words' as she encourages people to write a new chapter in their personal life story. Her intimate connection to The Goddess ~ the Earth Mother and the messages that come from nature weave a path in the unity between mind, body, soul and emotions to form the foundations of her business.

www.judedownes.com
www.facebook.com/gatewaytothewisewoman

OTHER TITLES BY JUDE DOWNES

From Grief to Goddess Book
From Grief to Goddess Healing cards

Gateway to the Modern Crone

www.ingramcontent.com/pod-product-compliance
Lightning Source LLC
Chambersburg PA
CBHW072047290426
44110CB00014B/1584